Kid Chemistry

Written by
Sandra Ford Grove and Dr. Judi Hechtman

Illustrator: Catherine Yuh

Editor: Karen P. Hall

Project Director: Carolea Williams

Table of Contents

Introduction

The lessons in this resource are designed to provide you with all the information you need to offer meaningful, hands-on scientific explorations with minimal preparation and maximum results. Each lesson includes the following components.

Learning Outcome

At a glance, you can see how students benefit from the activity and the knowledge they will gain.

Process Skills

The process approach to science encourages divergent thinking and provides tools for students to learn about their world. The following process skills are highlighted in student explorations.

Investigating	Measuring
Predicting	Inferring
Observing	Collecting Data
Comparing	Recording Data
Classifying	Communicating
Experimenting	Constructing Models

Connections

Additional activity ideas help students connect science concepts to other curriculum areas and to their own lives. This section includes a school connection to extend learning across the curriculum and a home connection to encourage family involvement.

Materials

A complete list of easy-to-find materials keeps preparation time to a minimum. You may wish to send home the parent letter (page 5) requesting help collecting materials.

Exploration

Each exploration has been designed to challenge and teach primary students through active participation. The teacher's role is that of facilitator, providing opportunities for scientific discoveries and encouraging students to raise questions. Questioning strategies are an important tool to extend student explorations and discoveries. Each lesson includes a few suggestions to help you get started.

Conclusion

This section includes background information and expected results. It may be presented before the exploration to guide instruction or after for more open-ended discovery.

Getting Started

Classroom environment is an important part of any science unit. Following are some suggestions for creating a stimulating environment that will motivate and excite students to explore science concepts. It is equally important to encourage family involvement as you begin your unit. Suggestions for making a home connection are also included below.

Exploration Station

Designate an area in the classroom for students to explore independently. Free exploration time will help students become familiar with the materials. You may wish to include:

- various crystalline solids (salts, sugars)
- mixing solutions (oil, water, molasses, liquid soap)
- food coloring
- mixing containers
- magnifying glasses
- acid-base indicators (pH paper or red-cabbage water)
- acid-base reference chart
- periodic table

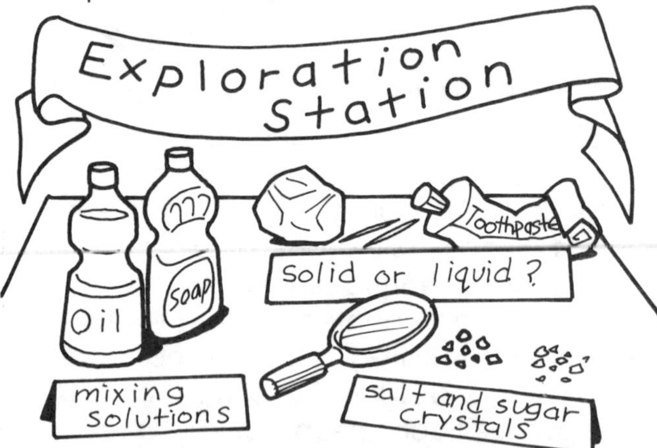

Home-School Connections

Encourage family involvement and parent communication by sending home the parent letter (page 5) at the beginning of the unit. Encourage children to share classroom activities at home, and invite parents to share in their child's learning experiences.

Learning Centers

Construct independent learning centers relating to chemistry. Activities for learning centers may include mixing solids and liquids, acid-base testing, and tie-dyeing shirts.

Bulletin Board

Dedicate a bulletin board in the classroom or hallway to science work. Display student diagrams, pictures, and writings from different explorations.

Literature Connections

Collect and display books about chemistry. Use the bibliography (page 32) for book suggestions. Ask the school librarian or visit your local library for additional help. Prominently display the books in your classroom for easy access. Display poems about chemistry on classroom walls.

Dear Family,

Our class is beginning an exciting science unit on chemistry. We will be investigating differences between chemical and physical reactions; acids and bases; and solutions, emulsions, and suspensions. As part of this unit, students will have assignments to complete at home. Share in your child's excitement and offer assistance whenever needed.

Some of the explorations involve materials you may have at home. If you can send any of these materials to class with your child, we would greatly appreciate it.

- paper plates
- plastic cups
- baby-food jars
- baking soda
- vinegar
- vegetable oil
- salt
- sugar
- food coloring
- aluminum pie pans
- margarine containers
- quart- and gallon-sized resealable plastic bags
- film canisters

We welcome guest speakers on subjects relating to chemistry. We would like to hear about topics such as careers in chemistry, famous chemistry discoveries, milk production, and chemistry "magic." If you, or anyone you know, would like to speak to our class, please contact me.

Our study of chemistry will be fun and exciting for everyone. Thank you in advance for being a part of your child's learning experience.

Sincerely,

Molecule Models

Learning Outcome

Students learn that all matter is made up of tiny particles called *atoms.*

Process Skills

- Students **construct models** of water and salt molecules.
- Students **compare** molecule models.
- Students **infer** that matter is made of different types of molecules.

Connections

★ **School**

Invite students to create "molecule monsters" with marshmallows and toothpicks. Have them give their creatures scientific names and write imaginative stories to describe their creations.

★ **Home**

Invite students and their families to create sugar-cookie molecules. Have them make different-sized, circular cookie-cutouts from the dough to represent different atoms and then connect the atoms together with dough strips to form molecules.

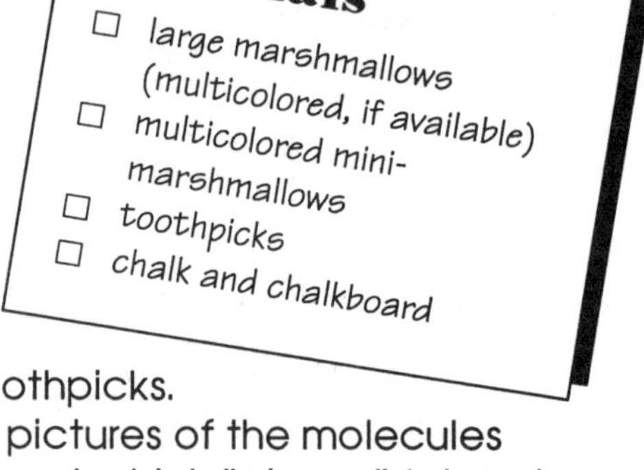

Exploration

Discuss atoms and molecules with students. Have students create water and salt molecule models (see illustrations below) by connecting small and large marshmallows with toothpicks. Guide students by drawing pictures of the molecules on the chalkboard, pointing out which "pieces" (atoms) are smaller (hydrogen and sodium) as well as the angle at which the atoms are attached. Have students use different-colored marshmallows to distinguish the four different atoms—hydrogen, oxygen, sodium, and chlorine. Invite students to share and compare their results.

- How do your molecules look similar? different?
- Why did we use different-colored marshmallows to make the models? Why not use the same size and color marshmallows for both water and salt molecules?
- How do you think hundreds of water molecules stick together to make water?

Conclusion

The smallest particles in nature are called *atoms.* They are considered the scientific "alphabet," combining together to form molecules of water, salt, and all other matter in our universe. Marshmallow models simulate how different atoms bond together to create familiar substances. Extend learning by inviting students to create salt-crystal models. Have them connect four salt molecules together through sodium/chlorine bonds (not sodium/sodium or chlorine/chlorine). Explain that, in real life, billions of salt molecules bond this way to create one salt crystal.

What's the Change?

Learning Outcome

Students learn the difference between a physical and a chemical change.

Process Skills

- Students **predict** whether tasks will cause physical or chemical changes.
- Students **investigate** and **classify** physical and chemical changes.
- Students **communicate** their results through writing and discussion.

Connections

★ **School**
Prepare with students two healthy snacks—one illustrating a physical change (such as cut fruit), the other involving a chemical change (such as baked banana bread).

★ **Home**
Invite students and their families to classify dinner items as those involving physical changes or chemical changes. Have students record their findings in a "meal log" for three days and then share their results with classmates.

Materials

- ☐ toast
- ☐ clay
- ☐ lab sheet (page 8)
- ☐ student test items (newspaper, orange slices, apples, ice cubes, bread, oil, vinegar, napkins, paper cups)
- ☐ teacher test items (matches, candle, newspaper)
- ☐ plastic knives
- ☐ baby-food jars

Exploration

Discuss the difference between a physical and a chemical change. Use toast to illustrate a chemical change—one in which an object is permanently altered. Show how molding a piece of clay is an example of a physical change—it's still clay regardless of the shape formed. Give partners lab sheets and test items. Ask them to predict and test whether items undergo physical or chemical changes. Have students observe you perform tests 3 and 4. Ask them to record their findings on their lab sheets.

- Which items went through physical changes? Why do you think so?
- Which items went through chemical changes? Why do you think so?
- What are some causes of physical changes? chemical changes?

Conclusion

A physical change such as slicing fruit involves altering the size, shape, or form of an object; the "identity" (molecular structure) of the object is unaffected. A chemical change such as burning paper permanently alters the molecular structure of an object; it is an irreversible process. Extend learning by discussing melting substances—a physical change. Show students how melted ice and wax can be refrozen and remolded back to their original forms.

Name ____________________ Date ______________

What's the Change?

	Predictions	Observations	Physical or Chemical Change?
1. Crumple a piece of newspaper.			
2. Tear a piece of newspaper.			
3. Watch the teacher burn newspaper.			
4. Watch a candle melt.			
5. Squeeze an orange slice.			
6. Cut an apple in half and check it after 15 minutes.			
7. Watch ice melt.			
8. Cut bread into pieces.			
9. Shake oil and vinegar together in a baby-food jar.			
10. Fold a napkin.			

Blue Goo

Learning Outcome

Students learn that some substances have characteristics of both solids and liquids.

Process Skills

- Students **experiment** with Blue Goo.
- Students **observe** movement of Blue Goo and **compare** it to solids and liquids.
- Students **record** their findings and share their results with classmates.

Connections

★ **School**

Prepare bread or cookie dough for students to explore and compare to Blue Goo. Discuss how "food thickeners" such as flour and cornstarch change the consistency of liquids. Invite students to make shapes with their dough and observe how it solidifies when baked.

★ **Home**

Send home the Blue Goo recipe for students to make and share with their families.

Materials

- ☐ measuring cup
- ☐ water
- ☐ large bowl
- ☐ blue food coloring
- ☐ 16 oz. (454g) boxes of cornstarch
- ☐ newspaper
- ☐ pie pans
- ☐ small objects (paper clips, pennies, confetti, toothpicks)
- ☐ science journals

Exploration

In advance, make Blue Goo and cover work areas with newspaper. Discuss and review characteristics of solids and liquids. Divide students into groups of four, and give each group a pie pan of Blue Goo. Invite students to handle and explore the consistency of the substance. Have them place various small objects on top of the Blue Goo and observe what happens. Ask students to record their findings in science journals.

- What happens when you squeeze Blue Goo, then let go? What happens when you pull it apart?
- What happens when you place your hand gently on top of the Blue Goo? What happens when you place small objects on the surface?
- Do you think Blue Goo is a solid or a liquid? Why?

(Note: Dispose of Blue Goo in the trash because it clogs sinks. Blue Goo turns to powder when dry, making it easy to clean off carpets.)

Conclusion

Blue Goo is an example of a non-Newtonian fluid—a substance that exhibits characteristics of both solids and liquids. Extend learning by creating a class chart comparing Blue Goo to various solids and liquids.

Borax Blobs

Learning Outcome

Students learn that force and pressure can change the consistency of some non-Newtonian substances.

Process Skills

- Students make and **experiment** with Borax Blobs.
- Students **observe** and **compare** how Borax Blobs react to various manipulations.
- Students **communicate** their findings through discussion.

Connections

★ **School**

Invite students to write imaginative stories about Borax Blobs. Encourage them to be creative, describing in detail how their blobs move and mold into different shapes throughout the adventure.

★ **Home**

Invite students and their families to make Borax Blobs. Have them compare Borax Blobs to other non-Newtonian fluids in their homes such as toothpaste, fingerpaint, and pudding.

Materials

- ☐ distilled water
- ☐ large bowl
- ☐ measuring cup
- ☐ Borax laundry booster
- ☐ wooden spoon
- ☐ newspaper
- ☐ small cups
- ☐ coffee stirrers
- ☐ individual glue bottles

Exploration

In advance, pour distilled water in a bowl—one ounce (28 ml) of water per student. Add Borax to the water until no more dissolves (a supersaturated solution). Cover work areas with newspaper. Give each student one ounce (28 ml) of Borax solution in a cup, a coffee stirrer, and a glue bottle. Ask students to squeeze small amounts of glue into the liquid and mix with coffee stirrers. Have them discuss what they observe (a blob forms instantly). Ask students to remove the blobs from their cups and knead them into smooth, dry balls. **Caution students to keep Borax away from their eyes and mouths.** Have students mold, pull, and squeeze their blobs.

- What happens to the thickness of the blob when you begin to knead and mold it?
- What happens when you pull the blob gently? roughly? shape it and bounce it like a ball?
- Do you think your creation is a solid or a liquid? Why?

Conclusion

Borax Blobs are examples of non-Newtonian solutions, possessing characteristics of both solids and liquids. They react to the forces of pushing and pulling, becoming more resistant and less able to flow. Borax Blobs contradict the claims made by Sir Isaac Newton who believed that only temperature could change the viscosity (thickness) of a liquid. Extend learning by inviting students to compare Borax Blobs with other non-Newtonian fluids such as Blue Goo (see page 9), putty, and toothpaste.

Water Wonders

Learning Outcome

Students learn how the chemical composition of water gives it unique properties.

Process Skills

- Students **investigate** the properties of water.
- Students **observe** the attraction between water molecules.
- Students **collect** and **record data** related to their investigations.

Connections

★ **School**

Have students investigate insects that use surface tension to walk on water. Invite students to write imaginative stories about these "water-walkers."

★ **Home**

Invite students and their families to investigate other liquids that behave the same way as water. Have them repeat the penny experiment using liquids such as cooking oil, milk, and rubbing alcohol.

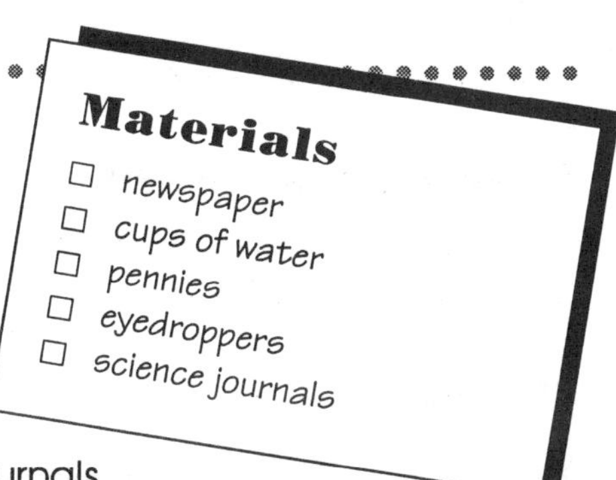

Materials

- ☐ newspaper
- ☐ cups of water
- ☐ pennies
- ☐ eyedroppers
- ☐ science journals

Exploration

In advance, cover work areas with newspaper. Give each student a cup of water, an eyedropper, and a penny. Ask students to predict in their science journals how many drops of water they think their pennies will hold. Have them gently add drops of water to the pennies, counting the drops added until surface tension breaks and water spills over the sides. Ask students to record the number of water drops and draw sketches of what they observed. Invite students to repeat the activity to improve their "scores."

- How many drops did you predict would fit on the penny? Did your prediction match your results?
- Were you surprised by your results? In what way?
- Why do you think the water drops stayed on the penny rather than immediately rolling off?

Conclusion

Students discover that water drops form a "bulge" on the penny rather than rolling off. This is because water molecules are polar—they have positive and negative sides causing them to attract and "stick" to each other. When too much water is added, surface tension breaks and the water disperses. Extend learning by having water-drop races on waxed paper. Invite students to draw racetracks and place waxed paper on top. Have them use toothpicks to pull water drops through the tracks.

Solution or Mixture?

Learning Outcome

Students learn to distinguish mixtures from solutions.

Process Skills

- Students **investigate** what happens when two substances are mixed together.
- Students **compare** characteristics of mixtures and solutions.
- Students **infer** the characteristics of mixtures and solutions by experimenting with a variety of substances.

Connections

★ **School**

Have students create snacks that are mixtures (trail mix) and solutions (lemonade).

★ **Home**

Invite students and their families to classify dinner items as mixtures and solutions. Have students write names or draw pictures of their grouped items and share their findings with classmates.

Materials

- ☐ paper cups
- ☐ testing items (water, oil, vinegar, molasses, baking soda, sand, sugar, salt)
- ☐ baby-food jars
- ☐ plastic spoons
- ☐ adhesive labels
- ☐ crayons or markers
- ☐ science journals

Exploration

Divide the class into partners, and give each pair cups of testing items, four empty baby-food jars, and four plastic spoons. Have students use the jars to combine pairs of testing items such as oil and water, oil and vinegar, and sugar and water. Ask them to label jars and secure lids before shaking the enclosed items together. Let the jars sit undisturbed for a few minutes, and then have students observe what happens in each one. Ask students to categorize jars into two groups—those with items that separate into layers and those with items that remain blended. Have them write descriptions and draw pictures of their results in science journals.

- Which ingredients combine, then separate into layers?
- Which ingredients blend to form one liquid?
- What do you think would happen if you combined more than two items together?

Conclusion

Substances that blend together to form a homogeneous liquid are called *solutions.* Substances that combine but separate into layers over time are called *mixtures.* Components in mixtures retain their own properties—components in solutions do not. Extend learning by inviting students to combine three or more ingredients together and observe the results. Also discuss and show examples of supersaturated solutions in which undissolved solid separates from the liquid.

Catch a Rainbow

Materials

- ☐ aluminum cookie sheets
- ☐ vegetable oil
- ☐ water
- ☐ smocks
- ☐ oil-based paints
- ☐ craft sticks
- ☐ straws
- ☐ white construction paper
- ☐ masking tape
- ☐ paper towels

Learning Outcome

Students learn that oil and water do not mix.

Process Skills

- ▶ Students **experiment** with immiscible materials to create art.
- ▶ Students **observe** that oil and water do not mix.
- ▶ Students **communicate** their results through artwork.

Connections

★ School

Invite students to write poems about rainbow colors and use paint-covered paper as background for a bulletin-board display.

★ Home

Invite students and their families to repeat the activity at home and use the oil-based designs as greeting cards or wrapping paper. For extra fun, invite students and their families to create "wave jars." Have them combine oil, water, and blue food coloring in a jar; secure the lid; and tilt the jar to create wave action.

Exploration

In advance, place cookie sheets at different work stations—one sheet for every two students. Lightly coat cookie sheets with oil, and fill them with water. Divide the class into partners, and give each pair smocks to wear, oil-based paints, craft sticks, straws, white construction paper, masking-tape strips, and paper towels (for cleanup). Have partners use craft sticks to add small drops of paint to the water pans. Ask them to blow on the floating paint drops with straws to make colorful designs. Have them attach masking-tape handles to opposite ends of white paper and then lower the paper until its surface gently touches the water's surface. After three seconds, ask students to lift the paper and observe the colorful results.

- What happened when you added the paint to the water? Why?
- What happened when you placed the paper on top of the water? Why?
- Do oil and water mix together? How do you know?

Conclusion

Students observe that oil-based paint floats on water. This occurs because oil and water are immiscible—they do not mix and will separate into layers. Students also discover that paper lifts paint from the water's surface. Extend learning by inviting students to test whether floating oil-based paint adheres to other materials such as foil, plastic wrap, waxed paper, and cloth strips. (Note: Discard oily water in a container rather than pouring it down a drain.)

Colorful Chromatography

Learning Outcome

Students learn that colored inks contain different-sized molecules.

Process Skills

- Students **experiment** with chromatography techniques to identify colors combined in various water-soluble inks.
- Students **predict** which colors will separate out of water-soluble ink.
- Students **observe** and **compare** colors separated through chromatography.

Connections

★ **School**

Invite students to discover how plants absorb water. Have them place fresh-cut, white carnations in cups of water tinted with food-coloring. Have students observe the white carnations turn color over the next few days.

★ **Home**

Invite students and their families to repeat this activity at home. For extra fun, invite students and their families to make tie-dyed shirts and model them for classmates.

Materials

- ☐ tall, clear-plastic cups
- ☐ water
- ☐ coffee filters cut into strips
- ☐ pencils
- ☐ transparent tape
- ☐ rulers
- ☐ black, water-soluble markers

Exploration

In advance, pour 1/2" of water into plastic cups. Divide the class into partners, and give each pair a cup of water, a coffee-filter strip, a pencil, a strip of tape, a ruler, and a black marker. Have partners tape one end of their filter strip to the center of a pencil, adjusting the length of the paper to match the length of the cup. Ask each pair to draw a thin black line 1" from the bottom of the filter strip. Have students lay the pencils across the tops of the cups to hang the paper strips into the water. Have students observe the ink as the water travels up the filter strip. When the strip is completely soaked, ask students to pull the strips from the cups and observe the results.

- What happened when you put the filter strip in the water?
- What happened to the black line? Why?
- What colors do you see on your wet filter paper? Where did they come from?

Conclusion

Students observe water moving up the filter through capillary action, separating the colors in the ink line. Inks and dyes are combinations of colors, with each color molecule having its own distinct size and shape. As diluted color molecules travel up the filter paper, they separate and travel at different speeds, depending on their size and shape. Extend learning by having students test other colors and brands to see which water-soluble ink produces the best results.

Goody Goody Gumdrops

Materials

- ☐ small bowls of flavored powdered gelatin
- ☐ cups of water
- ☐ eyedroppers
- ☐ plastic forks
- ☐ science journals

Learning Outcome

Students learn that some solids mix with but do not completely dissolve in liquids.

Process Skills

- Students **predict** what will happen when drops of water are added to powdered gelatin.
- Students **observe** the suspension formed when water is added to powdered gelatin.
- Students **communicate** their results through writing, illustrations, and discussion.

Connections

★ **School**

Invite students to sample the different-flavored gelatin "gumdrops" and graph the class favorites.

★ **Home**

Invite students and their parents to create and compare "gumdrops" to gelatin molds. Have students observe how heating the water causes the gelatin to dissolve.

Exploration

Divide the class into partners, and give each pair a bowl of powdered gelatin, a cup of water, an eyedropper, and a fork. Have students slowly add ten drops of water to the same spot in the gelatin, allowing each drop to completely absorb before adding the next. Ask students to predict and record in science journals what the gelatin "gumdrops" will look like when removed from the bowl. Have students use forks to gently lift and observe the wet gumdrops. Ask students to draw pictures of their gumdrops in science journals. Invite students to make more gumdrops and compare the shapes formed.

- What happens when powdered gelatin gets wet?
- What does the wet gelatin look like in the bowl? out of the bowl?
- What shapes are your "gumdrops"? What do they taste like?

Conclusion

Students create gelatin suspensions by adding water to powdered gelatin. A suspension is formed when a substance mixes with but does not dissolve in a liquid or gas. Extend learning by inviting students to experiment and create other suspensions, using water and substances such as flour, dirt, cornstarch, and glitter.

Stick to It

Learning Outcome

Students discover that some materials chemically combine to create sticky substances.

Process Skills

- Students **experiment** with liquids and solids to create different pastes.
- Students **measure** and **compare** the strengths of created pastes.
- Students **record** their findings in science journals.

Connections

★ **School**
Invite students to use favorite pastes and paper scraps to create colorful collages or papier-mâché art.

★ **Home**
Invite students and their families to explore and discover different glues and pastes at home and in local stores. Have them list household items which are partly or entirely held together with paste or glue. Invite students to share their findings with classmates.

Materials

- ☐ dry cooking ingredients (cornstarch, flour, sugar, oatmeal, salt)
- ☐ newspaper
- ☐ plastic spoons
- ☐ cups of water
- ☐ eyedroppers
- ☐ paper cups
- ☐ coffee stirrers
- ☐ labels
- ☐ paper scraps
- ☐ science journals

Exploration

Cover work areas with newspaper. Divide the class into partners, and give each pair cups of dry ingredients, plastic spoons, a cup of water, an eyedropper, empty paper cups, and coffee stirrers. Explain to students they are to create pastes by mixing water with various dry ingredients. Brainstorm characteristics of a good paste and ways to test how well pastes work. Have students mix spoonfuls of ingredients and drops of water in paper cups. Ask them to label their cups, writing the kind and amount of each ingredient used. Invite students to test their pastes on paper scraps. Have them record their results in science journals.

- What properties do we look for in a good paste?
- What ingredients make sticky paste? Which do not?
- How do you rate your pastes? Which is the best? the worst? Why?

Conclusion

Students discover that certain substances such as cornstarch and flour make sticky pastes when mixed with water, whereas other materials such as salt and sugar do not. Students also discover the consistency and strength of pastes differs depending on the amount of dry and wet ingredients combined. Extend learning by creating a class chart comparing different paste strengths. Have each pair check pasted papers after 15, 30, and 60 minutes to compare and rank durability.

Creative Teaching Press, Inc.

Little Miss Muffet

Learning Outcome

Students learn how milk curdles to form curds and whey.

Process Skills

- Students **predict** what will happen when vinegar is added to milk.
- Students **observe** milk curdling to form curds and whey.
- Students **communicate** their results through drawings and discussion.

Connections

★ **School**

Brainstorm foods made from milk such as cheese, butter, and yogurt. Discuss how milk products provide calcium needed for strong, healthy bones.

★ **Home**

Invite students and their families to make cottage cheese by mixing 3 tablespoons of lemon juice with 2 cups buttermilk and stirring the mixture over low heat until it curdles. Have parents use colanders lined with cheesecloths to separate the curds of cheese from the liquid whey. Invite them to add small amounts of whipping cream and salt to taste.

Materials

- ☐ small baby-food jars
- ☐ whole milk
- ☐ paper cups
- ☐ vinegar
- ☐ tablespoon
- ☐ "Little Miss Muffet" poem
- ☐ crayons or markers
- ☐ science journals

Exploration

In advance, prepare for each student a baby-food jar filled with whole milk and a paper cup containing two tablespoons of vinegar. Read together "Little Miss Muffet," and tell students they will make their own curds and whey.

Distribute jars of milk and cups of vinegar. Ask students to pour the vinegar into their jars, secure the lids, and swirl the jars to mix the ingredients. Let the jars sit undisturbed for three to four minutes. Ask students to observe what happens and draw their results in science journals.

- What happens to the milk when you add vinegar?
- Do you think milk alone would show the same results? Why or why not?
- What part of the mixture do you think is the curd? the whey?

Conclusion

Students discover that milk curdles when mixed with vinegar. The large clumps of curdled milk are called *curds.* The remaining liquid portion is called *whey.* Extend learning by repeating the investigation with lowfat, skim, and nonfat milk. Invite students to share and compare results.

Unbeatable Butter

Learning Outcome

Students learn how butter is formed from coagulated cream.

Process Skills

- Students **investigate** how to make butter.
- Students **observe** liquid cream turning to solid butter.
- Students taste and **compare** the textures and flavors of homemade butter.

Connections

★ **School**

Read aloud *From Grass to Butter* by Ali Mitgutsch. Invite students to create a mural of the pasteurization process.

★ **Home**

Invite students and their families to visit a dairy farm to see how milk is collected and processed. Have students and their families make homemade butter to use in favorite recipes. Invite students to share their creations with classmates.

Materials

- ☐ ice chest
- ☐ pint-size cartons of whipping cream
- ☐ small baby-food jars
- ☐ flavorings (salt, onion powder, garlic powder, brown sugar, honey)
- ☐ plastic knives
- ☐ crackers

Exploration

Keep whipping cream chilled in an ice chest until you're ready to begin this activity. Divide the class into partners, and give each pair a baby-food jar and a flavoring (optional). Distribute a carton of whipping cream to every four students, having pairs take turns filling their jars ⅓ full with cream. Invite students to add flavoring to their cream before securing the lid tightly to the jar. Have partners take turns shaking their jars vigorously until solid butter is formed (approximately five minutes). Invite students to spread butter on crackers and taste and compare their results.

- What happened to the cream in the jar after shaking it?
- How do you think liquid cream changed to solid butter?
- What does your butter taste like? How does it compare to butter made by your classmates?

Conclusion

Students observe liquid cream turn to solid butter. The shaking action breaks the coating of fat particles in the cream. These fat particles then stick together (coagulate) to form butter. Extend learning by inviting students to compare the amount of solid butter formed to the amount of liquid cream remaining in the jar. Have students estimate how much whipping cream would be needed to make a pound of butter.

How Sweet It Is!

Learning Outcome

Students discover that regular and diet soda differ in chemical composition.

Process Skills

- ▶ Students **observe** and **compare** the behavior of diet and regular soda through various tests.
- ▶ Students **infer** that artificial sweetener and sugar differ in chemical composition.
- ▶ Students **record** their findings in science journals.

Connections

★ School

Explore and investigate with students the canning process. Discuss how chemicals (preservatives) are added to keep canned and frozen foods from spoiling.

★ Home

Invite students and their families to conduct taste tests, identifying canned drinks made with artificial versus natural sweeteners. Have students share results with classmates.

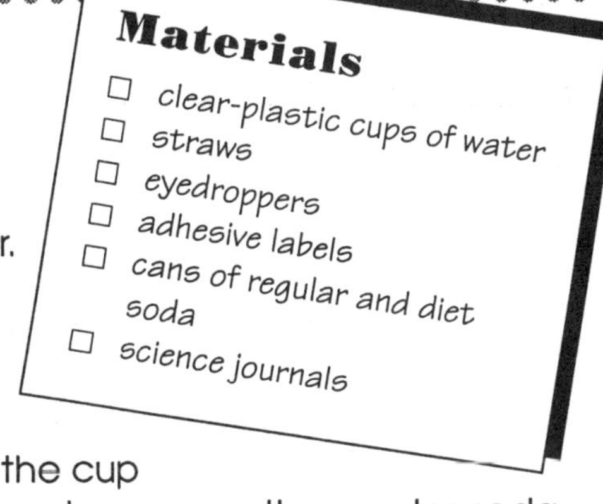

Materials

- ☐ clear-plastic cups of water
- ☐ straws
- ☐ eyedroppers
- ☐ adhesive labels
- ☐ cans of regular and diet soda
- ☐ science journals

Exploration

Give partners two cups of water, two labels, two straws, and an eyedropper. Have each pair label one cup *Regular* and the other *Diet*. Ask them to place a straw in the *Regular* cup so it touches the cup bottom at an angle. Have partners open the regular-soda can and use an eyedropper to add soda through the top of the straw into the water. Ask them to carefully remove the straw from the cup without stirring the liquids and to observe how the soda and water mix. Have students rinse the eyedroppers and repeat testing using the *Diet* cups and diet soda. Ask students to compare results and record their findings in science journals.

- What happens when you add drops of regular soda to water?
- What happens when you add drops of diet soda to water?
- Do you think regular and diet soda are made from the same chemical ingredients? Why or why not?

Conclusion

Although artificial sweeteners and natural sugars taste similar, they differ in chemical composition. This is apparent when students compare mixtures of soda and water. They observe that regular soda mixes readily with water whereas diet soda does not. Extend learning by inviting students to repeat testing with other regular and diet drinks. Have them test carbonated and noncarbonated liquids to see if results are different.

Alka Poppers

Learning Outcome

Students learn that some chemical reactions involve the release of gas.

Process Skills

- Students **predict** how many times a canister lid pops off due to buildup of carbon dioxide.
- Students **observe** a chemical reaction with Alka Seltzer tablets.
- Students **measure** the time it takes for canister lids to pop.

Connections

★ **School**
Discuss how plants need carbon dioxide to survive. Explore with students uses for carbon dioxide including yeast, soft drinks, and fire extinguishers.

★ **Home**
Place supplies in resealable plastic bags, and invite students to repeat the activity at home with their families. Invite students to share their experiences.

Materials

- ☐ Alka Seltzer tablets
- ☐ empty film canisters
- ☐ small cups of water
- ☐ eyedroppers
- ☐ science journals

Exploration

In advance, break Alka Seltzer tablets into pieces (about six per tablet), and place a piece in each film canister. Give each student a canister containing Alka Seltzer, a cup of water, and an eyedropper. Have students put on safety goggles and add just enough water drops into the canister to cover the Alka Seltzer. Have students quickly place lids tightly on the canisters, stand back, and observe what happens. Tell them to recap the canisters as soon as the lids pop off. Have students predict and record how many times their lids pop off before the solution inside stops fizzing. Ask students to measure and record the time periods between each pop.

- What happened to the Alka Seltzer when you added water?
- Why do you think the lid popped off?
- How many times did the canister lid pop off? Did each pop take more or less time to occur? Why?

Conclusion

Alka Seltzer combined with water fizzes and releases carbon dioxide gas. Lids pop off the canisters due to built-up pressure from carbon dioxide. As time passes, less carbon dioxide is released and the frequency of "popping" is reduced. Extend learning by graphing class results. Invite students to repeat the process with uncapped containers to see and hear the chemical reaction taking place.

Rising Raisins

Learning Outcome

Students learn that combining baking soda and vinegar creates carbon dioxide.

Process Skills

- Students **investigate** how to create carbon dioxide by mixing baking soda and vinegar with water.
- Students **observe** raisins rising on carbon dioxide bubbles.
- Students **communicate** their results through drawings and discussion.

Connections

★ **School**

Invite students to measure how many times a raisin rises and falls in one minute. Create a class graph of the results.

★ **Home**

Invite students and their families to repeat this activity using carbonated drinks such as soda pop or seltzer water.

Materials

- ☐ newspaper
- ☐ small cups of vinegar
- ☐ small cups of baking soda
- ☐ clear, plastic cups half-filled with water
- ☐ raisins
- ☐ plastic spoons
- ☐ science journals
- ☐ crayons or markers

Exploration

In advance, cover work areas with newspaper. Divide the class into partners, and give each pair vinegar, baking soda, water, three raisins, and a plastic spoon. Ask students to observe what happens when they place raisins in the water. Have them add a level spoonful of baking soda to the water and note any changes. Ask students to add a spoonful of vinegar and observe what happens to the raisins. Have them add more vinegar as needed until they observe the raisins floating in the solution. Have them draw pictures of their results in science journals.

- What happens to the raisins when you drop them into a cup of water? Do the raisins float or sink?
- What happens when you add baking soda to the cup?
- What happens to the raisins when you add vinegar to the cup?

Conclusion

Vinegar mixed with baking soda causes the formation of a gas called *carbon dioxide*. Students observe carbon dioxide bubbles form around the raisins causing them to float. As the bubbles break, the raisins sink to the bottom of the cup. Extend learning by inviting students to see how other solid objects (peanuts, popcorn kernels, pencil shavings) interact with the carbon dioxide bubbles in the cup.

Enzyme Investigations

Learning Outcome

Students discover the effects of oxygen on cut fruit.

Process Skills

- Students **investigate** the chemical effects of oxygen on cut fruit.
- Students **observe** and **compare** vitamin C-treated fruit and untreated fruit exposed to air.
- Students **communicate** their findings through writing and discussion.

Connections

★ **School**

Invite students to explore and discover how dried fruit is made. Invite students to carve faces in apples and observe what happens after the apples sit uncovered for a week.

★ **Home**

Invite students and their families to make fresh fruit salad, adding small amounts of lemon or orange juice to prevent discoloration. Have students explain and show family members what happens when cut fruit is left untreated.

Materials

- ☐ apples
- ☐ plastic knives
- ☐ paper plates
- ☐ vitamin C tablets
- ☐ resealable plastic bags
- ☐ rolling pins (or baby-food jars)
- ☐ science journals

Exploration

Divide the class into partners and give each pair an apple, a plastic knife, a paper plate, a vitamin C tablet, a plastic bag, and a rolling pin. Have students place the vitamin C tablets in the plastic bags and use rolling pins to crush the tablets into powder. Ask students to cut their apples in half and sprinkle one piece with vitamin C powder. Have them place both halves on paper plates and let them sit uncovered for one hour. Ask students to check apples every fifteen minutes and record their observations in science journals.

- What happened to the plain apple piece after 15 minutes? 30 minutes? one hour?
- What happened to the vitamin C-treated apple piece?
- Would the results be the same if you placed the plain apple piece in a sealed plastic bag? Why?

Conclusion

Students discover that untreated apple pieces turn brown when exposed to air. This is due to oxygen in the air reacting with enzymes in the cut fruit. Treated apple pieces do not darken because the citric acid in the vitamin C reacts with the fruit enzymes, preventing oxygen from taking effect. Extend learning by exploring how citrus fruit juice can stop cut fruit from turning brown. Invite students to experiment with various concentrations of lemon juice to see which works best.

Cent-sibly Green

Learning Outcome

Students discover that vinegar chemically reacts with copper to turn it green.

Process Skills

- Students **predict** what will happen when copper pennies are coated with vinegar.
- Students **observe** a green coating forming on pennies.
- Students **infer** that vinegar chemically reacts with copper in pennies.

Connections

★ **School**
Invite students to discover how vinegar chemically reacts with limestone (calcium carbonate) in rocks. Have students add drops of vinegar to various rocks and observe the fizzing that occurs in those containing limestone.

★ **Home**
Have students and their parents investigate chemicals in and around the home. Ask parents to discuss the hazards of these chemicals, safety precautions, and emergency procedures to follow if an accident occurs.

Materials

- ☐ paper towels
- ☐ pennies
- ☐ margarine tubs
- ☐ cups of vinegar
- ☐ science journals

Exploration

Divide the class into groups of three, and give each group two paper towels, eight pennies, a margarine tub, and a cup of vinegar.

Ask students to fold paper towels into fourths. Have them place one towel inside the margarine tub and the other alongside the tub. Ask students to pour just enough vinegar in the tub to soak the paper towel. Have each group place four pennies on the vinegar-soaked towel and another four pennies on the dry towel. Let the pennies sit undisturbed overnight. Ask students to observe and record their results in science journals.

- What happened to the pennies placed on the vinegar-soaked towel?
- How did vinegar-soaked pennies look compared to pennies placed on the dry towel?
- Do you think a chemical reaction occurred between the vinegar and the pennies? Why?

Conclusion

Students observe that vinegar-soaked pennies turn green whereas pennies placed on dry paper towels do not. Acetic acid in vinegar reacts chemically with copper in pennies to produce copper acetate, a green-colored substance. Extend learning by inviting students to test and compare results of soaking pennies in other acidic liquids such as lemon juice and grapefruit juice.

Ice Fishing

Learning Outcome

Students learn that salt affects the freezing temperature of water.

Process Skills

- Students **investigate** what happens when salt is sprinkled on ice cubes.
- Students **observe** how salt helps string adhere to ice.
- Students **communicate** their findings through drawings and discussion.

Connections

★ School

Have students investigate the salt content in oceans. Invite them to explore plants and animals that have adapted to saltwater environments. Discuss how oceans must be less than 32 °F (0 °C) to freeze due to salt in the water.

★ Home

Invite students and their families to test and compare freezing points of plain and salty water. Have them place paper cups filled separately with plain and salty water in the freezer and then check cups every half hour to see which water freezes first.

Materials

- ☐ small paper plats
- ☐ 1 ft. (30.5 cm) string pieces
- ☐ bowls of water
- ☐ ice cubes
- ☐ salt packets
- ☐ plastic spoons
- ☐ paper plates
- ☐ crayons or markers
- ☐ science journals

Exploration

Give each student a paper plate, a piece of string, a bowl of water, an ice cube, and salt. Have students dip their ice cubes in water and place them on paper plates. Ask each student to lay one end of the string across the top of the cube. Have him or her sprinkle small amounts of salt over the top of the ice cube and string. Have students slowly count to ten and observe what happens to the ice cubes when they gently lift the free end of the strings. Ask students to draw pictures of their observations in their science journals.

- What happened when you poured salt on the ice?
- What happened when you lifted the string? Why do you think this happened?
- Why do you think salt is poured on icy streets during winter weather?

Conclusion

Students observe the string stick to the ice cube. The salt reacts with ice, lowering its freezing point and causing the ice to melt. As the melted water dilutes and "overpowers" the effects of the salt, it refreezes over the string. Extend learning by inviting students to "fish" for ice cubes in a glass of water using string and salt.

Ice Cream in a Bag

Learning Outcome

Students learn that temperature can influence chemical and physical reactions.

Process Skills

- Students **investigate** how cold temperature affects liquids and solids.
- Students **observe** liquid cream turn to solid ice cream.
- Students **communicate** their results through discussion.

Connections

★ **School**
Take a class poll on favorite ice-cream flavors. Invite students to graph and illustrate the results.

★ **Home**
Invite students and their families to make homemade ice cream following classroom procedures or using an ice-cream maker. Encourage students to make different-flavored ice cream to share with classmates.

Materials

- ☐ quart- and gallon-sized plastic zipper bags
- ☐ ice
- ☐ ice chest
- ☐ ice cream ingredients (whipping cream, sugar, vanilla)
- ☐ measuring cups and spoons
- ☐ cups of rock salt
- ☐ plastic spoons

Exploration

In advance, fill gallon-sized plastic bags 1/3 full of ice—one bag for every three students. Store the bags in an ice chest. Divide the class into groups of three, and give each group ice-cream ingredients, measuring cups and spoons, a quart-sized plastic bag, and a cup of rock salt. Ask each group to measure and pour 1 cup whipping cream, 1/4 cup sugar, and 1/4 tsp. vanilla into their plastic bags. Have them seal the bags tightly and shake to mix the ingredients. Have each group place the small, sealed bag inside an ice bag and add 1/2 cup salt to the ice. Ask students to seal the ice bags and take turns shaking them to mix and cool the enclosed ice-cream ingredients. Have students drain the melted water out of the ice bags when necessary. Ask students to observe what happens to the cream mixture over time. Invite students to taste their results.

- What happened to the chilled, creamy liquid?
- Why is ice important for making ice cream?
- Why do you think salt was added to the ice?

Conclusion

Whipping cream absorbs the cool moisture released by melting ice, causing it to freeze and form ice cream. Salt melts the ice quicker, releasing more cool moisture to freeze the cream. Extend learning by inviting students to add small amounts of flavored syrup to the ingredients to make flavored ice cream.

The Power of Sour

Learning Outcome

Students learn that radishes can be used to test the acid content of foods.

Process Skills

- Students **investigate** the acid content of various foods.
- Students **observe** a color change when using radish juice as an acid-base indicator.
- Students **communicate** their results through writing and discussion.

Connections

★ School

Explore and investigate with students acid rain. Discuss how it is created and how it affects the environment. Invite students to test different water samples in the community for acid content.

★ Home

Invite students and their families to test the acid content of liquids found in their kitchens. Have them compare and share their results with classmates.

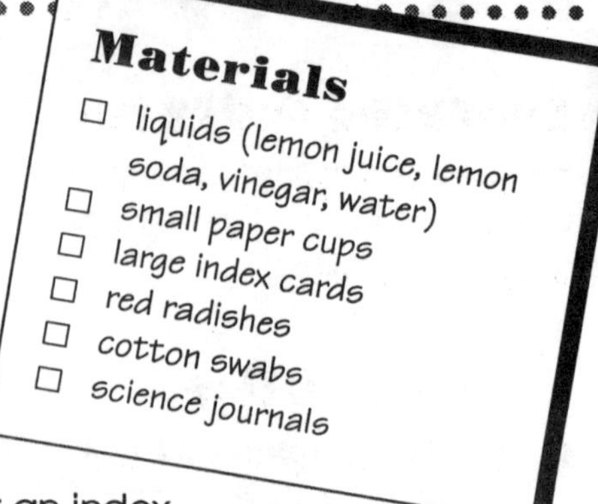

Materials

- ☐ liquids (lemon juice, lemon soda, vinegar, water)
- ☐ small paper cups
- ☐ large index cards
- ☐ red radishes
- ☐ cotton swabs
- ☐ science journals

Exploration

In advance, pour small amounts of lemon juice, lemon soda, vinegar, and water in separate labeled paper cups—one set for each pair of students. Divide the class into partners, and give each pair an index card, a radish, a set of liquids, and four cotton swabs. Ask partners to rub the radish on the card to make four moist "indicator" spots. Have students write in pencil under the spots *Lemon Juice, Lemon Soda, Vinegar,* and *Water* to match the four liquids being tested. Ask students to use separate cotton swabs to apply corresponding liquids to the test spots. Have students observe any color changes and record their findings in science journals.

- What color was each "indicator" spot before adding the liquids? after adding the liquids?
- Which liquids caused the spots to change color?
- If acidic substances turn radish juice dark red, which of the liquids contain acid? Which do not? How do you know?

Conclusion

Students observe that acidic substances such as lemon juice and vinegar turn the radish juice dark red whereas neutral or basic liquids such as water do not. Lemon soda, a diluted acidic solution, causes only a slight color change. Extend learning by inviting students to test the acidic content of other liquids such as a baking soda/water solution, dish-washing detergent, or rainwater.

A Solid Study

Materials

- ☐ labels
- ☐ paper cups
- ☐ solids (cornstarch, flour, sugar, salt, baking soda, instant mashed potatoes)
- ☐ liquids (iodine, water, vinegar, juice from boiled red cabbage)
- ☐ investigation kits (six black-paper squares, one magnifying glass, four eyedroppers, and six sheets of waxed paper per kitt)
- ☐ lab sheets (page 28)

Learning Outcome

Students discover how various solids and liquids react when mixed together.

Process Skills

- ▶ Students **experiment** with mixtures of solids and liquids.
- ▶ Students **observe** and **compare** solids reacting with liquids.
- ▶ Students **collect** and **record data** on lab sheets.

Connections

★ School

Invite students to investigate healthy and unhealthy foods containing starches and sugars. Discuss daily food choices and a well-balanced diet.

★ Home

Invite students and their families to repeat food testing at home using artificial sweeteners, instant pudding mix, cake mix, and various spices. Have students make a chart of their results and share their findings with classmates.

Exploration

In advance, prepare labeled cups of solids and liquids—one set (six solids, four liquids) per group of four students. Distribute investigation kits and lab sheets. Have student groups pour small amounts of each solid on separate paper squares. Ask them to look at the solids through magnifying glasses and record their observations on their lab sheets. Invite students to mix solids and liquids, one solid at a time. Have them pour four small piles of the solid on a sheet of waxed paper and add drops of different liquids to each pile. (Be sure students use different eyedroppers for each liquid.) Have students observe and record their results. Ask students to repeat testing with other solids.

- How are the solids similar? different?
- Which liquids react with each solid? How do you know?
- Why do you think scientists perform these tests?

Conclusion

Some solids and liquids change color when mixed together. Iodine turns purple or black when mixed with starches. Red-cabbage juice turns yellowish-green when mixed with bases, and bright red when combined with acids. Other solids and liquids such as vinegar and baking soda fizz when combined. Extend learning by inviting students to mix three or more solids and liquids together.

Name ______________________ Date ______________

A Solid Study

Directions: Look at and feel each of the following ingredients, and record your observations on the lines below.

Sugar ______________________

Flour ______________________

Cornstarch ______________________

Baking Soda ______________________

Instant Mashed Potatoes ______________________

Salt ______________________

Directions: Mix pairs of solids and liquids together. Write *C* for those that show a color change, *F* for pairs that fizz, and *D* for those that dissolve or "melt" together. Write *none* for mixtures that show no reaction.

	Sugar	Flour	Cornstarch	Baking Soda	Instant Mashed Potatoes	Salt
Iodine	C					
Water						
Vinegar						
Red-Cabbage Juice						

Real-Life Connections

As each science topic is studied, make real-life connections to professional, community, and family life:

- Invite a dietitian to discuss chemistry involved in food preparation.
- Visit a bakery to discover how ingredients combine through chemical reactions to make baked goods.
- Invite a guest speaker to talk about and demonstrate food-dehydration techniques.
- Invite a chemist to show how chromatography is used to determine the composition of plants.
- Invite a pharmacist to talk about his or her profession.
- Invite an artist to demonstrate using food-dyes.
- Invite a policeman to discuss crime-scene chemistry.

Culminating Activity

Invite students to demonstrate their knowledge of chemistry by hosting a chemistry luncheon for their families and friends. Have them prepare foods that involve chemical and physical changes, mixtures, solutions, and emulsions such as baked goods, mayonnaise, butter, salad dressing, and ice cream. Invite students to give each food a creative chemistry title. Have them create and print menus that include the chemistry involved in making each food. For extra fun, invite students to use chromatography-colored filters to make paper flowers, and oil-based painted paper to make decorations and place mats.

Assessment

An important goal in early childhood science education is to generate curiosity and enthusiasm about science. In a hands-on program, students should receive credit for participation and involvement as well as comprehension.

Rubric

A rubric is a scoring guide that defines student performance. Use the Performance Evaluation and Rubric (page 31) to assess student progress for each exploration.

Portfolios

Student lab sheets, journals, and self-evaluations are important parts of science portfolios. All portfolio entries should be dated so they can be chronologically compared at any time. Teacher checklists and performance evaluations can also be helpful in keeping track of progress and achievements.

Anecdotal Records

Keep written records of observations that verify students' understanding of science concepts and processes during hands-on activities. Use these to assist in student and parent conferencing.

Student Conferences

Ask students to discuss their most interesting exploration. Guide them using questions such as: *What did you learn by doing this exploration? What might you do differently if you tried it again?*

Name ______________________________ Date ______________

My Science Work

Exploration: ______________________________

My work was:

My best! | Good. | I can do better.

By doing this exploration, I learned ______________________________

____

____

If I could do it again, I would ______________________________

____

Performance Evaluation

Student ________________________________ Date ____________________

Check the level that best reflects student's performance.

Exploration: ______________________	**Performance Level** Excellent	Very Good	Good	Needs Improvement
Shows motivation and curiosity for learning.				
Draws reasonable conclusions from science exploration.				
Demonstrates full understanding of concepts.				
Clearly communicates and listens to others.				
Accurately records and describes observations.				
Uses knowledge to solve problems or extend thinking.				
Comments:				

Rubric

Excellent

Goes beyond competency, adding creativity and insight to overall performance. Shows initiative and takes charge of learning. Listens attentively to others. Shows advanced critical thinking skills. Written work is polished with detailed explanations that extend into other subject areas.

Very Good

Uses skills effectively. Listens well during discussions, contributing thoughtful ideas and opinions. Work is neat and accurate, showing evidence of higher-level thinking. Does not take risks or extend ideas into other subject areas.

Good

Shows much effort and desire to learn but is still working on mastery of skills. Written work is accurate but shows little creativity or higher-level thinking. Follows directions well but needs extra encouragement and time to organize work.

Needs Improvement

Lacks organization and effort. Student is unsure of how to use materials or uses them incorrectly. Written work is inaccurate and shows little or no creativity. Does not follow directions and needs additional guidance to perform general tasks.

Bibliography

Children's Books

Beech, Linda. *The Magic School Bus Gets Baked in a Cake: A Book about Kitchen Chemistry.* Scholastic, Inc., 1995.

Cole, Babette. *The Slimy Book.* Random House, 1986.

dePaola, Tomie. *The Popcorn Book.* Holiday House, Inc., 1978.

Hale, Lucretia. *The Lady Who Put Salt in Her Coffee.* Harcourt Brace Jovanovich, 1989.

Hurwitz, Johanna. *Russell Sprouts.* Puffin Books, 1989.

Steig, William. *Gorky Rises.* Farrar, Straus, and Giroux, 1986.

Van Allsburg, Chris. *Two Bad Ants.* Houghton Mifflin Co., 1988.

Zemach, Harve. *Salt.* Farrar, Straus, and Giroux, 1977.

Resource Books

Challoner, Jack. *The Visual Dictionary of Chemistry.* DK Publishers, 1996.

Cobb, Vicki. *More Science Experiments You Can Eat.* J.B. Lippincott, 1979.

Cobb, Vicki. *Science Experiments You Can Eat.* J.B. Lippincott, 1972.

Williamson, Sarah and Zachary. *Kids Cook! Fabulous Foods for the Whole Family.* Williamson Publishing Co., 1992.